MW01623160
THIS BOOK BELONGS TO:
JUDAICA PRESS KIDS

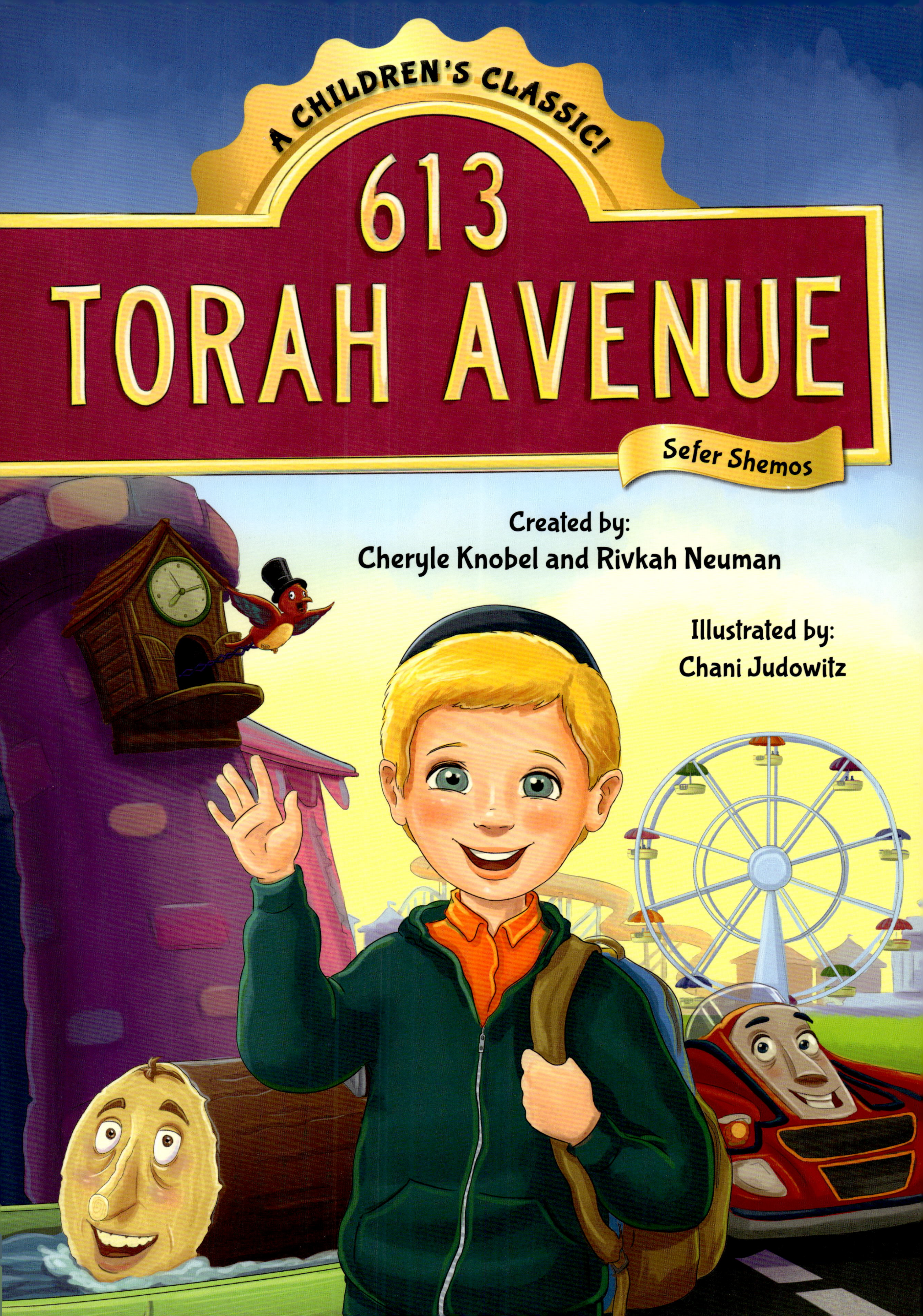
A CHILDREN'S CLASSIC!
613
TORAH AVENUE
Sefer Shemos
Created by:
Cheryle Knobel and Rivkah Neuman
Illustrated by:
Chani Judowitz

This book is based on the 613 Torah Avenue parsha series that was produced many years ago and remains popular to this day.

Firstly, we would like to express our gratitude to Hashem for providing us with the inspiration for this timeless classic, now transformed into print.

A special thank you to Shabsie Knobel and Rabbi Moshe Neuman for their continuous support and encouragement.

Sincere gratitude to Nachum Shapiro of Judaica Press for his role in coordinating all aspects of this project.

Thank you to Rabbi Shmuel Klein of Torah Umesorah for his genuine concern in encouraging the continuation of the 613 Torah Avenue series in book form.

Much appreciation to Chani Judowitz for her outstanding illustrations and creativity. Her enthusiasm and understanding of children's interests ensured the success of this project.

Thanks to Rabbi Shmuel Kunda, a"h, for his unique creativity, and to Yisroel Lamm for his wonderful musical arrangements.

— Cheryle Knobel and Rivkah Neuman

Dedicated to Dovid: May you be zocheh to always love Torah and mitzvos and continue to be a source of light and joy to all. — Chani Judowitz

613 Torah Avenue — Sefer Shemos

ISBN: 978-1-60763-301-3

Created by: Cheryle Knobel and Rivkah Neuman
Illustrations: Chani Judowitz
Cover and internal design and layout: Nachum Shapiro
Proofreader: Chaim Schneider

THE JUDAICA PRESS, INC.
123 Ditmas Avenue / Brooklyn, NY 11218
718-972-6200 / 800-972-6201
info@judaicapress.com
www.judaicapress.com

Manufactured in China

CONTENTS

Please note: This book contains pesukim from the Torah and should be treated respectfully.

"It's me, your friend Chaim. I'm here once again.
We met once before — remember when?
The last time that we met
Was on Torah Avenue. How could you forget?
But today, everyone here is just delighted,
And I'm also so excited.

This great amusement park has opened nearby
With rides, and games, and great things to try.
I brought some sandwiches and a little bentcher,
And I'm on my way to a new adventure.

All this excitement makes my head ring,
So, to stay calm, I think I'll sing."

It's time to learn Torah right now.
Follow me — I'll show you how.
If every one of us tries,
We will grow up great and wise.

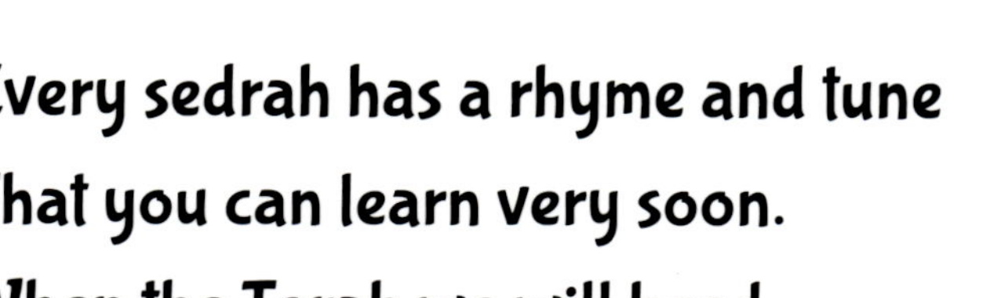

Every sedrah has a rhyme and tune
That you can learn very soon.
When the Torah we will heed,
We are bound to succeed.

"Wow, this place is really gigantic,
With people running all over, so frantic.
It's so huge, it gets me nervous ...."

"*Uh-huh!* It's Klutzy the Clown, at your service!"

"Hey, who are you and from where did you appear?"

"*Huh-huh!* I'm the guy with the brains around here.
I can answer any question. *Huh-huh,* I never fail,
Because my head is as sharp as a rusty nail."

"All right, let me ask this of you:
How much is two and two?"

"*Guuh* ... two and two equals toot!
The sound you make when you play a flute."

"Now answer this: When do we eat
hamantaschen that we love?"

"*Uhh,* that we eat on Tisha B'Av!"

"No, no! Tisha B'Av is a day to fast!"

"Fast? I run very fast ... In every race I come in last!"

"Oh, please! At least tell me
what you do on Chanukah."

"On Chanukah? *Ha-ha!* I play with my harmonica!"

"Oh, no! So when do we eat latkes, piping hot?"

"*Uuh,* that should be on, *uh,* Tu B'Shvat!"

"Oh, well. Tell me, do you know which country
had a king called Pharaoh?"

"Well, of course! Ha-ha, that was Mexico!"

"Maybe you can tell me, please,
Which nation was enslaved by Pharaoh's decrees?"

"I know, *huh-huh* — it was the Japanese!"

"As sure as my name is Chaim,
The Jews were slaves to Pharaoh in Mitzrayim."

**Each man worked as a slave.
The Jews were beaten but were brave.
"All boys born must be
Drowned" was Pharaoh's decree.**

**The Jews were sad when this they heard,
But they didn't listen to Pharaoh's word.
A boy was born and hidden for a while,
Then his basket put into the Nile.**

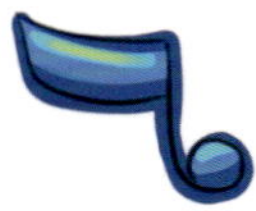

**Miriam stood nearby
As Pharaoh's daughter heard a cry.
She saw the basket, and she knew
This lovely baby was a Jew.**

**"'Moshe' he'll be called," said Pharaoh's daughter,
For he was taken from the water.
As Moshe in the palace grew,
Of B'nei Yisroel's suffering he knew.**

"Good-bye, Klutzy, I'd better look for something else to find
Before you make me lose my mind."

"Come one, come all! Come down this way
To Meshulem Magician's matinee!
It's only ten cents admission
To see the world's greatest magician.

Look here, folks, there's a fish in this bowl,
And with one swish … it turns into a gefilte fish!
Now, let me cover this fish with my hat
And now it'll turn into a … cat! *("Woof!")*

"Oh, no, he messed it up!
Instead of a cat, I see a pup!"

"Oh, my, that pup made me look like a fool!
They'll throw me out of magic school!"

"Don't feel bad, Meshulem. I can tell you one thing:
You should be working for Pharaoh the king.
He had magicians with all sorts of tricks,
Like making snakes out of sticks.
Until Moshe came and got his stick ready,
And it ate all those snakes up like strings of spaghetti."

SHEMOS

B'nei Yisroel suffered bitterly.
Moshe was seen killing a Mitzri.
From Mitzrayim Moshe fled.
Yisro's daughter then he wed.

As Moshe watched the sheep one day,
A baby lamb ran away.
He followed the lamb and saw
A bush burning more and more.

Moshe heard Hashem tell him
To lead the Jews from Mitzrayim.
Moshe and Aharon told Pharaoh,
"Let the Jews go!"

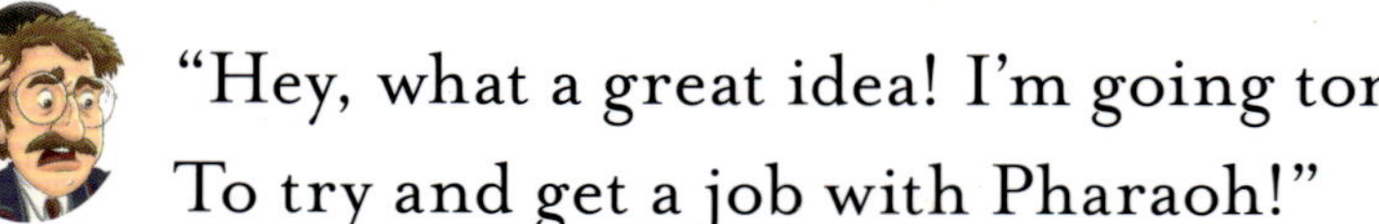

"Hey, what a great idea! I'm going tomorrow
To try and get a job with Pharaoh!"

"Good luck, Meshulem, on your new career.
Meanwhile, I think I'll disappear."

"This place is so confusing and new —
Not at all like quiet Torah Avenue.
Look, there's a ride called the Flume!
I'll get into this hollow log,
and into the water I'll zoom.
Move, log, move — where's your pep?
Go, log, go — don't be a shlep."

"Shiver, shiver, how I quiver ...
The water's so cold inside this river,
It gives me goosebumps on my liver."

"What a strange thing to be —
Sitting inside a talking tree!"

"Oh, why couldn't I have been used
to make a bicycle
Instead of freezing in this water like an icicle?
They couldn't make me into a wooden spoon?
A spool, a house, a wooden broom?"

"You should be happy, Mr. Log. You really should.
You talk like your head is made of wood.
This water is so fresh and not one bit muddy,
Not like in Mitzrayim where all the water
turned bloody."

"Boy, that would be like trying to swim across
A river of tomato sauce!"

"That's right, Mr. Log,
And after the blood was gone
came frog after frog."

VA'ERA

"The water is blood!" all did shout.
Frogs were jumping in and out.
Bugs were crawling everywhere.
Rrr! Wild animals were a scare.

Then came Dever, by and by.
All the farm animals died.
Sh'chin – boils, and pimples, too,
On the Mitzrim, not the Jews.

Ten Makkos, Makkos ten.
The Mitzrim were punished
Again and again. (2x)

Barad was fire and hail.
In Mitzrayim, a loud wail.
Grasshoppers, flying quick.
Then the darkness, very thick.

Makkas Bechoros was the last.
Pharaoh ran to Moshe fast.
He was afraid to die, so ...
He said, "Let those Jews all go!"

Ten Makkos, Makkos ten.
The Mitzrim were punished
Again and again. (2x)

"Hey, that song really tickled my bark.
I should be happy working in this amusement park.
So watch out down below ... here I go!"

"Riding on you, Mr. Log, was really great, you bet.
But my shirt, tzitzis, shoes, yarmulke, socks, and underwear are soaking wet!
So it's time to see what more
Fantastic adventures are in store."

דָּם
צְפַרְדֵּעַ
כִּנִּים
עָרוֹב
דֶּבֶר
שְׁחִין
בָּרָד
אַרְבֶּה
חֹשֶׁךְ
מַכַּת בְּכוֹרוֹת

"Come one, come all! Come run, don't crawl.
C'mon and try to throw this ball.
Pinky Platsky is my name,
And hitting that circle is the game.
If you hit that red circle over there,
You win this big stuffed teddy bear!"

"And what do I win if I hit it twice?"

"You'd win this five-pound bag of rice!"

"And what if I hit it eight times or nine?"

"You win this big stuffed porcupine!"

"Okay, here's your dime, and now the pitch. ...
I hit the red circle! I'm rich!"

"Very good — here's your teddy.
Try it twice if your aim is steady. ...
Wow, he hit it twice!
Here's your five-pound bag of rice. ...

He hits it every time he tries!
He's taking every single prize!
Please stop! Stop pitching it in!
I have nothing left for you to win!"

RICE
RICE

“Oh, I couldn’t carry this home — it’s much too heavy.
It would take a Buick or a Chevy.
Not like in Mitzrayim, when the Jews were told
To take along the silver and gold.
When they left Mitzrayim, they had donkeys and oxes
To carry their bags, their crates, and their boxes.
Now, at last they were free,
After so many years of slavery.”

BO

**The tenth Makkah was fulfilled –
Each firstborn Mitzri was killed.
Over the Jews Hashem passed.
It was time to go at last.**

**Moshe told the people to prepare.
Yetzias Mitzrayim was near!
There was no time to bake bread.
They put dough on their backs instead.**

**To remind us we were saved,
Chag HaPesach Hashem gave.
In Mitzrayim, slaves were we.
Then B’nei Yisroel were set free.**

“I’ll be on my way now. I just can’t wait
For some more adventures that are first-rate.
There’s more to see — there’s a whole new part
Where you ride around a track on a little go-kart!
Look at those go-karts zooming past!
They’re going at least 97 miles fast!”

“You’ll need lots of nerve and a very strong heart
To take a ride in this go-kart!”

“A talking go-kart? Let me get in and step on the pedal.
Maybe we can win the go-kart medal.
This you call fast? It’s barely a crawl.”

“Oy, something is making *mein* engine stall.”

“What’s wrong, Mr. Go-Kart — why don’t you feel right?
Such a brand-new go-kart of red and white.”

“Oy, this is no time for flattery
When I have a pain in my battery.
Not to mention the pain in my engine.
Please, would you help me if you could?
Do me a favor — open up my hood.
Look, right underneath my fenders
Someone left a pair of suspenders.”

“And to add to all this drama,
Here’s a clock, and a rock, and a green pajama!
No wonder you were sick with all that junk
Inside your motor instead of your trunk.”

GO-KARTS
RACE CAR TRACK
3

"What's that I see? It must be a dream!
A stand that sells all flavors of kosher ice cream!"

"This way, ice cream lovers, *huh-huh*, I'm the one
That sells ice cream with the flavors of *mun*."

"Klutzy the Clown selling ice cream? Is that you?"

"*Huh-huh*, of course! Now I'm doing something new.
Look at all these flavors that I have in stock!
With millions of colors it's yummy, *geshmak*!"

"Well, which type of ice cream should I try?"

"*Huh-huh*, why don't you try pizza pie?"

"Pizza ice cream? Please, do me a favor ...
Do you have a different kind of flavor?"

"Sure, we have string bean ice cream, or tomato,
Spinach ice cream, or mashed potato.
Any flavor of ice cream is yours to choose
Ha-ha! Like the *mun* that was eaten by the Jews.
The *mun* had the taste of almost any dish,
Or any food that you could wish."

BESHALACH

For days the B'nei Yisroel marched.
From thirst their lips were parched.
Of hunger the people complained.
"In Mitzrayim we wish we had remained."
***Mun* – a special food – was sent.**
To each it tasted very different.
One portion was gathered each day.
If more was taken, it rotted away.
In honor of Shabbos, on Yom Shishi,
Twice as much for each family.
Now we have *lechem mishneh*, and the reason why –
The double portion of *mun* that fell from the sky.

ICE CREAM
LAVORS
PIZZA
SOUP
BAGEL
FISH
MASHED
OTATO

"These flavors, like falafel or kugel,
it would seem,
Are fine for *mun*, but not for ice cream ...

Say, what's that over there? Is that a balloon,
Shaped like an apple, a pear, or a moon?
It's a little boy buying balloons over there.
The balloon man is filling them all up with air."

"Mr. Balloon Man, blow up the one
shaped like a salami,
And I'll give you a quarter from my mommy."

"Okay, okay, here's a red one shaped like a pear."

"Oh, look at that blue one over there!
Keep the green one. Keep the red.
I want the blue one to tie to my bed!"

"Okay, okay. ... Here, take it and go.
I have no more breath left to blow."

"Hey, that other kid has a yellow one
shaped like a banana,
With an orange map of Indiana!"

"Please, little boy, take the one that's blue.
I have no more banana ones left for you.
Take the blue balloon and be a good fellow."

"No, I want the one that's yellow!
No green, no red, no purple, no blue!
That kid has yellow — I want one, too!"

“Excuse me, little boy, I heard the way you began to scream and bellow,
Because someone else had one that was yellow.
In the Aseres Hadibros, the Torah did tell us:
If your friend owns something, don’t be jealous.
There are ten commandments, and this is one of them,
That Moshe brought down to us from Hashem.”

YISRO

I am your Hashem. I brought you from Mitzrayim.
No other shall you serve. My mitzvos observe.
You shall not use in vain Hashem’s holy name.
Remember the Shabbos day. Keep it a special way.

Honor your parents, too. Long life Hashem will give you.
You shall not kill – that is Hashem’s will.
You shall be moral and true. Believe in the mitzvos you do.
Do not steal when with others you deal.

False witness never be – you must live truthfully.

Don’t be jealous of your friend’s things – his toys or her pretty rings.
The Torah Hashem did give, a guide for us to live.
To Hashem always be true, because you are a Jew.

“I’m sorry. The way I acted was a shame.
From now on, I’ll try to behave much more tame.”

“Now you’re talking the way you should.
Be happy with what’s yours, and you’ll see that it’s good.

I think that it's time now to wash and eat lunch.
I'll sit down on this bench and start to munch.
Say, look at all these words and pictures and lines
That someone has scraped on this bench as design."

"I'm almost ready to scream and *plotz*
When people scratch words on me in different spots.
Words like "Hi, Barry," or "Melvin is a banana,"
Or "Harry is a Galitzyana."
All these phone numbers on me make me look
Like a New York City telephone book."

"A bench like you should be used to sit,
Not to write so many names on it.
It says in Mishpatim that no one is free
To damage another's property."

MISHPATIM

All the laws, the Mishpatim,
That Moshe Rabbeinu brought
To us from Har Sinai,
To Am Yisroel he taught.
"Na'aseh V'nishma" was our cry.
"We will do and we will hear, without asking why." (2x)

When dealing with our friends,
Being fair in work or play.
These laws taught by Moshe
Are with us today.
Midvar sheker tirchak –
Never tell a lie.
To keep away from sheker
We must always try.
"Na'aseh V'nishma" was our cry.
"We will do and we will hear, without asking why."

"My good lad, if there was an election, you'd be elected
The watchman to keep this place protected."

VIN IS A BANANA

"I'm off now, Mr. Bench, to that very large tent.
I don't have much time here left to be spent.
That very large tent is not yet complete.
They're trying to stretch that large canvas sheet
Over that pole that stands thirty feet.
Pardon me, sir. Why can't you prevent
The falling in of your beautiful tent?"

"I'ma working alla day with lotsa cement
Ana tools, ana machines that I had to rent
To try to put up thisa impossible tent.
I pull on the inside —
 she go down on the outside.
I pull on the northa side —
 she go down on the southa side.
I justa wish that someone would invent
An easy way to build a tent."

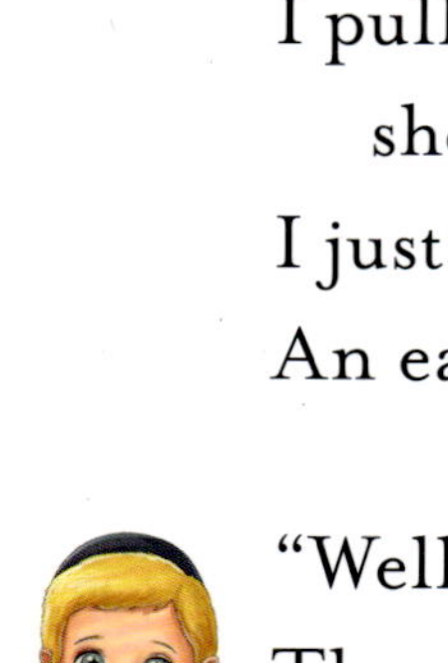

"Well, sir, do you know that in the desert where the Jews were sent,
They also built a most beautiful tent?
With the gold and silver that the Jews donated,
The Mishkan was built, as Hashem stated."

TERUMAH

Hashem said, "Build a Mishkan for Me,
So that among the Jews I'll be."
Gifts for the Mishkan they did bring.
There was a plan for everything.
They brought gold, and silver, too,
Wool of purple and of blue.
A Menorah made of gold so pure.
There were curtains for the door.
The Aron was covered in and out with gold,
The Luchos to hold.
The Shulchan was made of special wood.
In the Mishkan they stood.

"Well, good-bye, Mr. Workman, you're a hardworking gent.
Lots of luck in your work on your tent.
Say! There's something that makes me laugh.
Is someone taking a photograph?"

"Ah'm Mr. Picture. I can dress you from your head to your toes
In the craziest, funniest, silliest clothes —
Like a clown, or a can of baked beans,
A bottle of ketchup, or a washing machine,
A monkey, or a long-legged giraffe —
And then I snap your photograph.
Hurry, young man, you're really in luck!
I can dress you like a garbage man in a truck."

"Thanks, Mr. Picture. I don't want to sound mean,
But don't you have a costume a little more clean?"

"Why, your picture in this will be some surprise.
This outfit is only ten times your size!"

"Oh, please! We should always see that the things we wear,
Like the Kohanim's clothes, are given great care.
The *begadim* fit perfect. As a matter of fact,
They could not bring a *korban* if their clothes were not exact."

TETZAVEH

"V'atah tetzaveh,"
The Jews were told by Moshe.
To bring *shemen* for pure light,
For the Menorah to burn bright.

Aharon was chosen to be
The Kohen Gadol from Shevet Levi.
He wore many special things,
And a Choshen with gold rings.

The Choshen was made for him.
It had the names of the twelve Shevatim.
All the clothes had to fit just right.
He served Hashem with all his might.

Aharon was chosen to be
The Kohen Gadol from Shevet Levi.
He wore many special things,
And a Choshen with gold rings.

"Look! While you were singing, I got
Lots and lots of these super snapshots."

"Super snapshots? In this one,
you see my belt and my feet.
In this one, my teeth, my ears, and the street."

"Well, I can't help it. I'm not to blame.
My camera doesn't know how to aim."

Cuckoo! Cuckoo! Cuckoo! Cuckoo!

"Listen to that clock! It must ring every hour
From high above on that colorful tower."

Cuckoo! Cuckoo! Cuckoo! Cuckoo!

"There it goes. It's ringing some more.
But look! It's only a quarter to four.
And there's something really absurd —
A funny-looking cuckoo bird."

"Cook-cook! Yoo-hoo! Boo-boo! Yoo-hoo!"

"*Yoo-hoo, Boo-boo?* What about saying '*Cuckoo*'?"

"Each hour, I pop out to state
The weather and the date.
It's the 42nd of Octember,
One week after the 3rd of Divember.
The temperature is 200 degrees,
And five below zero if there is a breeze.
That is all I have to state.
I'm sorry if I sound *fahrdreit*."

"Mr. Yoo-hoo Bird, you haven't said one sensible word.
Your mixed-up date and information
Is like the mistake that was made by the Jewish nation.
When Moshe climbed Har Sinai, he told the Jews to wait
And that he would come back on a certain date.
But some of the Jews made the wrong calculation,
And they mixed up the date and the information."

KI SISA

The Jews were waiting. They counted the days wrong.
It seemed as if Moshe was away so long.
"Where is Moshe? We all want to know."
B'nei Yisroel cried to Aharon so.
Aharon told the Jews he wanted them to wait.
He knew that Moshe was not late.
He asked them all to bring jewelry of gold.
They quickly did all that they were told.
Aharon threw the gold and jewelry into the flame.
Then an Egel it became.
Moshe was angry at the Jews when he came down.
He dropped the Luchos onto the ground.

Moshe begged Hashem B'nei Yisroel to forgive.
Those that did teshuvah should live (2x)

"It's also an interesting lesson about time —
To waste it or lose it is surely a crime."

"Oh, Mr. Go-Kart, where are you and all your friends going this time?"

"It's getting late — don't you hear the clock starting to chime?"

Cuckoo, cuckoo, cuckoo, cuckoo ...

"Like all good things, I suppose,
Today's adventures must come to a close."

"I guess it is kind of late, but even if you are closing for the day,
I'll be back tomorrow anyway."

"I hatea to disappointa you, but tomorrow we'll be gone.
Our show must travel on and on.
We'll pack our bags and fold our tents
And travel on to new events."

"Oh, Mr. Workman, it's just like the Mishkan, which we are told
Was portable, and easy to fold.
It was carried with the Jews over desert sand
Until they came to the Promised Land."

"But whether we travel by car, bus, or train,
Whenever it's Shabbos, we stop, and there we remain."

"This is something the Torah states clearly.
Don't work on Shabbos — treat it dearly."

VAYAKHEL-PEKUDEI

**B'nei Yisroel gathered and they heard.
Moshe told them Hashem's word:
In six days all work you must do.
Shabbos is special for every Jew.
Even work for the Mishkan
On Shabbos Kodesh must not be done.
This job was done by Betzalel.
Gifts were brought by B'nei Yisroel.
They brought more than was needed
For the Mishkan to be completed.
Its purpose was fulfilled.
Now it was as Hashem willed.
When on the Mishkan the cloud appeared,
The people knew Hashem was near.
When the cloud lifted, they could see
They should continue on their journey.**

"But Mr. Go-Kart, Meshulem, Mr. Workman,
and Klutzy the Clown —
Does this mean you'll never be back in my town?
To think that you'll never be back over here
Is really more than I can bear."

"*Huh-Huh!* Don't worry, Chaim, have no fear —
We will all be back together next year.
Heh-heh, just keep on singing the Torah Avenue song,
And we'll be together before very long."

**It's time to learn Torah right now.
Follow me — I'll show you how.
If every one of us tries,
We will grow up great and wise.**

**Every sedrah has a rhyme and tune
That you can learn very soon.
When the Torah we will heed,
We are bound to succeed.**

Torah Umesorah Publications

620 Foster Avenue, Brooklyn, New York, 11230

Tel. 212-227-1000

Menachem Av 5779

I am among the countless individuals whose fondest memories of young parenthood include playing the "613 Torah Avenue" series to our children. The sounds and impressions of those wonderful productions still resound with my children many years later. The approach was novel back in the day; and I have no doubt that "613 Torah Avenue" served as a paradigm which others later emulated in their bid to infuse pure Torah values into children. The pleasant text and songs were—and continue to be—most impacting.

I was quite excited to learn that the producers of the original records are now coming out with a written version for children to read—and listen to... as the resource will be accompanied by CD's. I have skimmed through the galleys of the book and can already feel the delight that children will surely have from receiving the newest product of "613 Torah Avenue."

Mrs. Knobel and Mrs. Neuman have invested their hearts and souls in this work for years. I know it will yet again be among the strong "teachers" of genuine Torah values to the Jewish children of today and to-morrow. I am most pleased to add my endorsement to the venture, with the blessing that it will be as well received as the original version was.

Rabbi Shmuel Yaakov Klein
Director, Torah Umesorah Publications

I Can Be A
גבור
SARA BLAU
ILLUSTRATED BY MALKA WOLF

I Can Be A
זריז
SARA BLAU
ILLUSTRATED BY MALKA WOLF

I Can Be
מותר
SARA BLAU
ILLUSTRATED BY MALKA WOLF

I Can Be
בשמחה
SARA BLAU
ILLUSTRATED BY MALKA WOLF

I Can Be
מכיר טוב
SARA BLAU

I Can Make a
קדוש השם
SARA BLAU

I Can Be
דן לכף
זכות
SARA BLAU
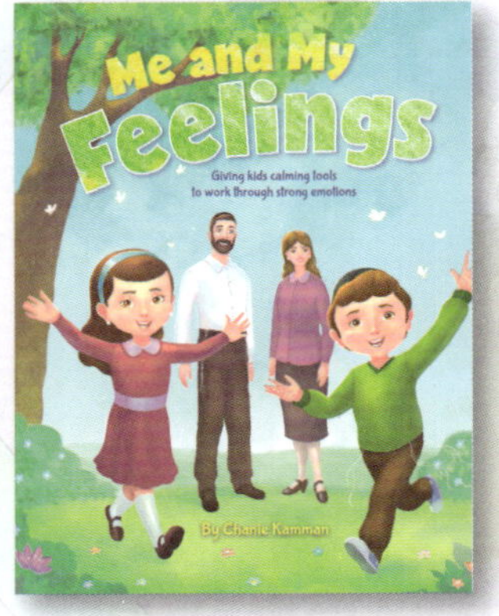
Me and My
Feelings
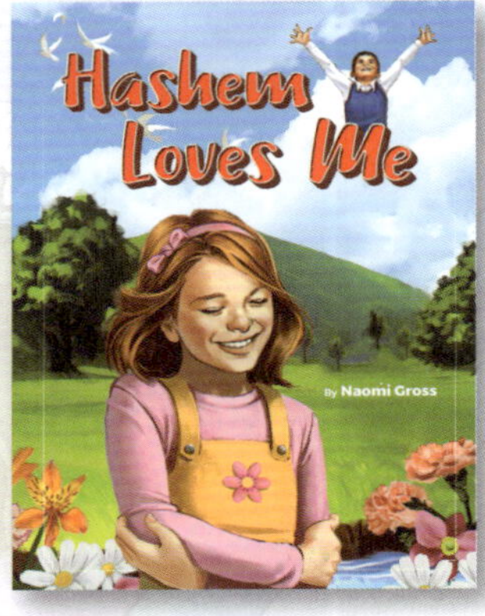
Hashem
Loves Me
By Naomi Gross

Let's Tell the Story of
The Beis Hamikdas
A child's first introduction
to Tisha B'Av
By Sara Blau
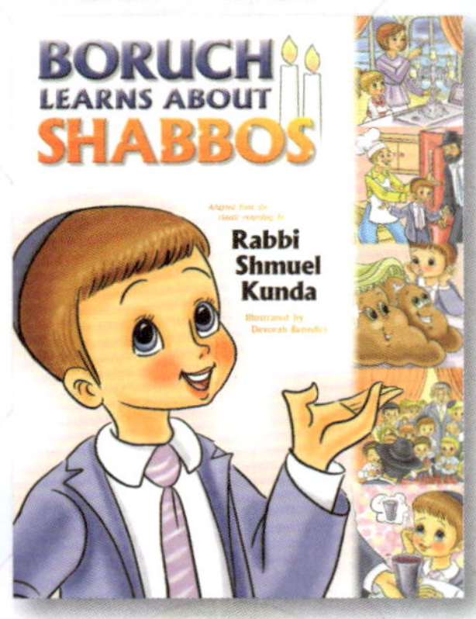
BORUCH
LEARNS ABOUT
SHABBOS
Rabbi
Shmuel
Kunda

BORUCH
LEARNS ABOUT
PESACH
By Rabbi Shmuel Kunda
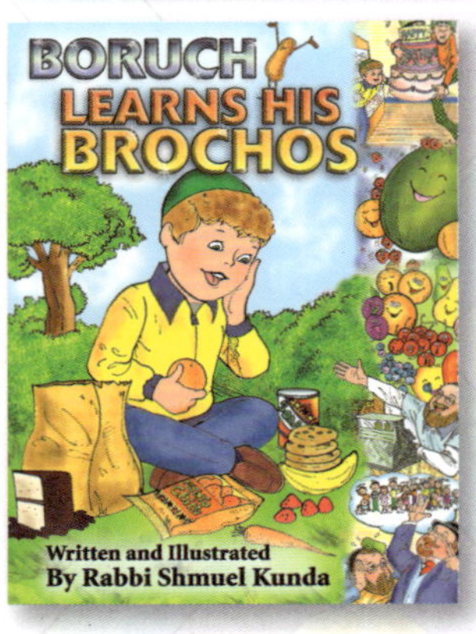
BORUCH
LEARNS HIS
BROCHOS
Written and Illustrated
By Rabbi Shmuel Kunda
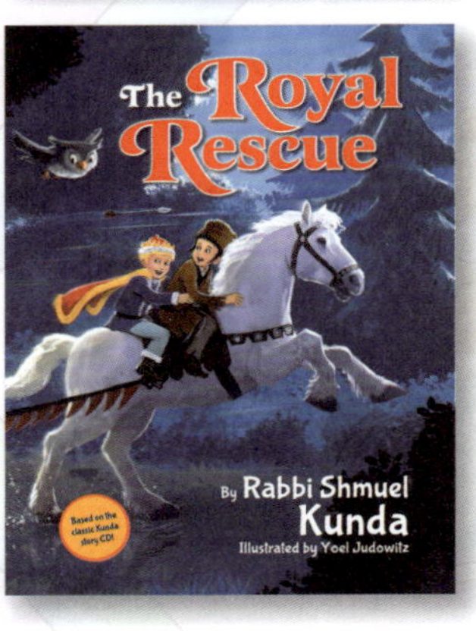
The Royal
Rescue
By Rabbi Shmuel
Kunda
Illustrated by Yoel Judowitz

Kunda Classics Collection
The Talking Coins
Rabbi Shmuel
KUNDA
Illustrated by
Boris Shapiro

Rabbi Shmuel Kunda
BORUCH
makes a
SIMCHA
Based on the classic Kunda story CD!
DURABLE
LAMINATED
PAGES!

Let's Appreciate
EVERYONE!
Bracha Goetz

MY VERY OWN
MITZVAH
MOUTH
BRACHA
GOETZ
ILLUSTRATED BY
MALKA WOLF

MY VERY OWN
MITZVAH
HANDS
BRACHA
GOETZ
ILLUSTRATED BY
MALKA WOLF
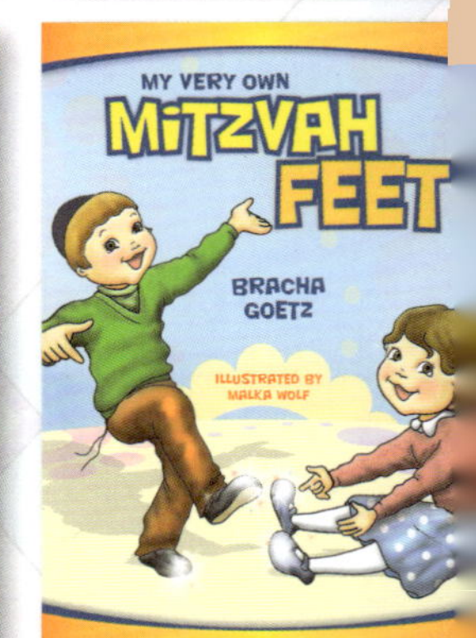
MY VERY OWN
MITZVAH
FEET
BRACHA
GOETZ
ILLUSTRATED BY
MALKA WOLF

Rachel Golan
Rivka Landa
3-Minute
Middos Stories for Children
(and Parents, Too!)
Illustrated by Roni Weiss
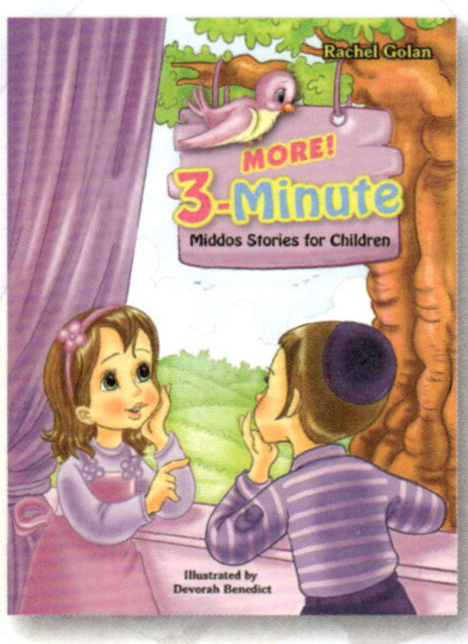
Rachel Golan
MORE!
3-Minute
Middos Stories for Children
Illustrated by
Devorah Benedict

The perfect introduction to Tefillah for kids!
I Daven
Every Day
by Naomi Shulman

A charming story that teaches kids how to take responsibility for their mistakes
My Sister
Has a Scooter
by Naomi Shulman

The perfect introduction to Tzedakah for kids!
I Give Tzedak
Every Day